WRITERS REPUBLIC

"Rocky Road" Survivors

RHUE ROSA

Copyright © 2021 by Rhue Rosa.

All rights reserved. No part of this book may be reproduced in any form or by any electronic or mechanical means, including information storage and retrieval systems, without permission in writing from the publisher, except by reviewers, who may quote brief passages in a review.

This publication contains the opinions and ideas of its author. It is intended to provide helpful and informative material on the subjects addressed in the publication. The author and publisher specifically disclaim all responsibility for any liability, loss, or risk, personal or otherwise, which is incurred as a consequence, directly or indirectly, of the use and application of any of the contents of this book.

WRITERS REPUBLIC L.L.C.
515 Summit Ave. Unit R1
Union City, NJ 07087, USA

Website: *www.writersrepublic.com*
Hotline: *1-877-656-6838*
Email: *info@writersrepublic.com*

Ordering Information:
Quantity sales. Special discounts are available on quantity purchases by corporations, associations, and others. For details, contact the publisher at the address above.

Library of Congress Control Number:		2021921910
ISBN-13:	978-1-63728-930-3	[Paperback Edition]
	978-1-63728-931-0	[Digital Edition]

Rev. date: 10/21/2021

Dedicated to my irreplaceable parents, Cosmo and Princess Layne, with love, honor and utmost respect.

Contents

Introduction

"Race me up the steps!"

I remember letting her win each time so that she could experience the thrill of victory daily, even on a small scale. I used to clamber up the staircase, deliberately lagging behind so that she could be the first to reach the top of the landing and breathlessly exclaim, "I win!". Then, the saga would continue as she raced to P.A.L. Head Start classroom 10, stealing furtive glances over her shoulder to see if I was catching up. She invariably arrived at the classroom door seconds before me and triumphantly announced to the teachers, "I won again!". The teachers pretended to commiserate with me, consolingly and condescendingly saying, "Mom, you need to try harder" (Although I am her step-grandmother, her teachers addressed me as "Mom" affectionately because I was being a mother to her during that time). I smiled each time and without missing a beat I'd respond, "Next time I'll win".

More often than not back in 2017 I kissed my step-granddaughter goodbye and headed to work reflecting on the period 22 years earlier when I was unable to move out of my hospital bed, much less race a 5 year old up the steps. In 1995 I would never have imagined that a time would come when a child would challenge me to push past obstacles and hurdles. Little did Angelina realize that each time she urged me on in her demanding 5 year old way, "Race me up the steps!", it was a call to rise to the occasion, to flex my mental muscles so that they wouldn't atrophy, to at least participate in the race of life so that when all is said and done I can have the assurance of knowing that I did take a step and kept going.

Every weekday morning began with that physical race to the top of a flight of stairs. But within each day there were also mini-races that involved interactions and interventions. Sometimes, I felt "winded" and it hurt to "breathe", but I recharged my batteries, regained momentum and kept going. I could have discouraged myself into a funk by dwelling on the fact that I was raising a precocious little girl, unrelated to me by blood, while simultaneously parenting my own biological children, juggling a full-time job and doing volunteer work in a community facing numerous challenges. I could have wallowed even deeper into the mire of my own personal "pity party" by harping on everything in my life that hadn't fallen into place when and how I expected.

But each morning when I embraced the summons, "Race me up the steps!", it served as a reminder that in spite of setbacks and disappointments, in spite of life events that are painful and unpleasant, in spite of moments that I feel powerless to affect change in a particular aspect of my life, I have made a conscious choice to keep moving forward. Somewhere along the line I had realized that it behooved me to implement a paradigm shift.

So...my step-granddaughter was not viewed as a nuisance- her rambunctiousness was spurring me to engage in physical activity which was nudging me closer to better health. The complex issues that our patients face are not overwhelming- they are fodder to steer me toward solution-oriented interventions. My work environment is ***not a graveyard where hope is buried- it's a garden that is flourishing***...first beneath the soil, but later, above ground where the life and vitality will be visible and palpable to all.

It's so profound that 5 words from the mouth of a 5 year old have had such an amazing impact on my life. For me, "Race me up the steps!" means don't crumble under the weight of adversity and affliction- persevere, endure, let the vulnerable "win" by empowering them to succeed. We ourselves actually "win" our daily races not when we cross the finish line first, but when someone else's life was enriched because of our touch, our words, our influence, our actions, our presence.

I firmly believe that someone with quadriplegia who can't move their limbs ***can move mountains***, a blind person ***can be a visionary***, a mute person ***can speak volumes***, an "ordinary" person can leave an ***extraordinary*** legacy behind. Strength is a term often used to define ***physical*** endurance...but I would broaden the application to describe those in our lives who motivate us to ***keep running, keep striving and keep trying***...those who inspire us to help others win, those who first empowered us by standing in our shadow so that we could bask in the glory of achievement. People such as these, like many of our loved ones, mentors, supervisors and administrators are the irreplaceable jewels that decorate the sidelines of this race called life.

Rhue Rosa, LMSW 7/27/17, updated 12/7/2020

Just On Our Own

you close your eyes and ears and ignore us
adults we expected to be there for us
you see us play ball and hang out
we smile and we laugh, we call out to girls as they
pass by...
but, our friends have died...
and we are forced to go on living
tho' we would've given anything
to reverse time...
hang out with "Man-Man" one more time,
argue with "D" over $2 one more time...
just on our own,
"day ones" vanishing like Vicks vapor right before our
eyes
'cause the playground is a battlefield when we step
outside
on the surface we're frozen but
burning up inside
'cause the support is lacking...
feelin' like no one has our back in
our time of sorrow
...yeah, "we Tilden boys be wildin' ", but we're human, not
hollow...
they don't see our potential...
they see thugs
so, no compassion, no hugs...

forced to heal our own wounds
from loved ones gone too soon
we can't even grieve how we need to, THEY were shot but
we're bleeding too!
can't start crying 'cause the tears would become a flood
if we shed tears for every son's shed blood,
sons *gone too soon* in the hood...
death is that unwelcome visitor, comes by without
warning
leaves families in mourning
So we're storming
the studio and letting our rage out
our bars can't remain caged... so we mic check then let
'em out
thru airwaves
and hope the airplay makes our names famous
so we'll be known for far more than just
being out here... *on our own*

in loving memory of "D"
4/25/2015 by Minister Rhue Rosa aka "Ma"

Poem inspired by E. T. (Brownsville resident); I dedicate
it to those who have survived trauma, grief, illness,
domestic violence.

Unsinkable

Unbreakable, I will NOT be submerged by pain
Unbreakable, greatness embedded in my name

Like bamboo I bend but I DON'T snap
Since childhood I endured wounds of life
Saw my mom cry, asked why, I pressed nevertheless
Wiped my tears and persevered past the strife

Like paper –when I was torn
I cut those who touched
The hurt in me seeped out in various forms
I was a shelter for the broken and extended myself
But had nowhere to run from MY personal storms

I gave in spite of my needs
putting others before me
Ending up empty, depleted and stained
But I've learned that I'm not a solitary note
I'm a symphony, a concerto, a joyful refrain!

I'm a wonder, I'm unique, I have a brilliant mind
I'm a magnificent, exceptional, Masterpiece on earth
And NO MATTER WHAT they call me or try to subtract
from me
The devil is a liar! They can NOT decrease my worth!

Unsinkable, I will NOT be submerged by pain
Unbreakable, greatness embedded in my name

By Minister Rhue Rosa, LMSW 1/5/2020

Diagnosed...Not Comatose

I have diagnoses...
but they're a mere part of me
I divorced depression
Broke up with anxiety

Physical abnormalities are not my totality.
Blood tests are so painfully inadequate to define me!
I had a purpose before the lab results came back
And I have value that no disease can subtract!

I've come to terms with the fact
that I'm diagnosed
BUT...I live, I move, I breathe
Clearly, I'm not comatose!

My medical record is
a Smithereen of my legacy
Even though I've decided that
Well-being is a priority

Chronic conditions can't
Undermine nor hinder the mission
diversions and distractions
Don't intercept my traction

In my peripheral vision
I see subliminal competition
Trying to compete for my attention
So that I won't mention...

my strengths, gifts and talents
The uniqueness that I represent
But, I love and value myself
And God runs my body's government!

By Minister Rhue Rosa, LMSW

Dedicated to people with HIV/AIDS, lupus, cancer, scoliosis and other health conditions

Forget the Folly...Fan the Flame!

In this day and age
The priority is social
So shall they focus on
Looking identical
Calling themselves worldly names
From the enemy
"Inner-me" calling the shots
And the scenery?...
Eerie backgrounds and backdrops
Too familiar...
Liars don't come at you straight
Stray "cats" lingering
Trying to distract and subtract
From my destiny
But I **remember His word**
So, I **forget the folly**
Lord, fan the flame of
The gift that's within me
Incinerate the ice cold
Feelings of apathy
Pathological mindsets depart

From my vicinity
Lord, fan into flame
My desire for the holy
Wholly dethrone flesh
And carnality
Lethal impulses and urges
Can't dwell in me
Telling me I can't succeed is INSANITY!
Forget the folly
The old me is history
Fan the flame and increase the mercury
No lukewarm vibe here
Warn them about consequence
Quench THESE flames???
I think NOT!!! devil, GO SOMEWHERE!!!
Like the lake of fire, satan,
Where YOUR future is
Die in pieces
While I rest in PEACE...with HIM!!!!!

By Minister Rhue Rosa 12/13/19

Loved and Lost

Wealth is not limited to the financial realm
Defined only by currency, dollars and cents
No...wealth includes the gain and the increase
The joy and the brilliance that they represent
Our loved ones have left...but memories remain
We've lost the visible... but love is eternal
We mourn and we weep,,, we grieve and we pause
Yet we persevere with a flame that's internal
We honor the VICTORS! They departed victorious!
They fought to the end and they WON our hearts
As we ponder and consider, reminisce and meditate
We are grateful and thankful for the support of S.T.A.R.

By Rhue Rosa, LMSW
Written on 9/25/2020
inspired by S.T.A.R. memorial

dedicated to those who lost loved ones to Covid-19

Well Life

Your name means "strong man".
You lived up to it-
Consistent, disciplined,
Grounded and rooted,
Steadfast and reliable...
You seldom fluctuated.
Even when work was challenging
You never hesitated.
Easy to get along with,
Sociable, good natured...
You believed in teamwork...
No time for hatred!
With the patience of Job
You mentored the novices.

You were equally at home in the field
Or in offices.
"Mr. Well Life"...what a lifetime well lived!
Those whom you encountered
Received precious gifts...
The desire to change,
Capacity to evolve
And the thrill of expansion
Due to you, Sir Carl!

Original poem written on June 29,2021
by Rhue Rosa, LMSW inspired by
Carl "Iron Dog" Stanbury

Our Atmosphere

We love our atmosphere
They say that Brownsville's trash, it's the worst
That only thugs and bums live here
So where we're at most fear
But we love Brownsville ...we love our atmosphere

I see broken men breaking records
Carrying loads of pain and heartbreak
From one morning 'til the next daybreak
Strong soldiers whose footsteps make the earthquake

I've seen mothers lose sons
And they weep...BUT they're warriors
Who wake up each day wondering what the day will
hold ...
they know life can slice and dice you like a ninja ... but
they don't fold

No, they fight to rise above depression and grief
There are women in Brownsville who wage war on their knees
Crying out to a God that their naked eyes can't see
Cuz they realize the devil lies but Jesus is real

We love our atmosphere
They say Brownsville's trash, that only bums live here
So where we're at most fear
But we love Brownsville...
We love our atmosphere

Dedicated to Brownsville, Brooklyn residents

Written by Minister Rosa 6:45am 12/17/2020

Stoner's Prayer

How high?
So high that I can touch the sky and ask Jesus,
"Why'd my loved one have to die?"
How high?
High enough to freeze the water in my eyes so the tears
won't flow like the River Nile...
I need to stay high enough that if my best friend drops
my heart won't stop
cause it'll be numbed up

you don't understand why I get high
Know what? I have no choice but to STAY high
I don't want to care, I don't want to feel...
I want to smoke till I make myself believe this isn't real
when I light up I'm power-FULL and pain-LESS,
able to tune out depression and stress
don't want the high to wear off
cuz I'll start dwelling on my loss...
loved ones buried in the dirt
wish I could bury my hurt
in a cemetery of memories
and be released from recent grief...
I can stop getting high?
I can? nah... this
can-na-bis

is my crutch, my cure, my open door
it leads me to the land of
"nothing phases me anymore"
But...
at this moment I'm recalling to mind
something unusual I heard as a child
I heard of someone they hung high and stretched wide.
how high?
so high that He could touch the sky ...
when they nailed His hands and feet and pierced His side.
how high?
so high that the grave couldn't hold Him.
every eye shall behold Him
at the appointed time...
and since i'm fiending for a hit
that wont fade away...I want to inhale LIFE
and see eternal days.
I want to exhale truth and make my friends get a
"contact"...
breathe that second hand gospel...sit back and watch the
impact...
do I need to wait to go to church to get saved? Hold up,
tomorrow isn't promised...I'ma just say a prayer...

Lord, forgive me, I'm a sinner and I'm so confused...no matter how high I get, can't get away from You!
if I spread my bed in hell You're right there...
even behind closed doors Your eyes are everywhere.
come into my heart, Jesus, before I wreck myself!
don't need these roll-ups anymore, just fill me with Yourself!
In spite of the chaos this will be a better year for me and I will hold my head HIGH in victory!!!

Original poem by Minister Rhue Rosa 12/29/14
Revised 9/30/20

Wanted

Spoken word inspired by God 6/11/2020
"You're under arrest!"...Arrested development.
That's what I see in the hood
I see talent apprehended and handcuffed
While headlines scream, "He's no good!"

First deprivation, now incarceration
Fatherless child stands before the judge
A few minutes of trial, not nearly enough time
To elaborate on the cause of his grudge

He knows from experience to remain silent...
Or here come MORE charges...of homicide
Cause he bored the judge and jury to DEATH
With details of dysfunction he faced as a child

Who wants to hear about sleepless nights?
About walking to school in fear of attack?
Countless days in dean's office, burning with rage
Generational curses like loads on his back

Expecting respect on a trek that leads nowhere
Because clothes can be changed, but not DNA
So, he breaks his neck to stand out from the masses
To be noticed, encouraged- not sent on his way

Now what can I do as a woman with no sons?
What can I say in the hood to the damaged?
I'll return you to "Sender", to God who created you
Through Christ you'll receive the power to manage

Strength to keep running past the temptations
Avoiding pitfalls and detours and cliffs
Spiritual sight...cause faith comes by hearing
Eyes of faith **see past time**...what are YOU working with?

The hood defies logic AND the laws of science
A grown man can "drown" in a 40oz of beer
Or commit suicide with some crack cocaine
No gun necessary...drugs and liquor are here

Did you know your life mattered **BEFORE** you were born?
BEFORE you left the womb you were set apart
You tried other techniques and everything failed
Time to let Christ sit on the throne of your heart!

By Minister Rhue Rosa, LMSW 6/11/2020

Walls and Wings

Written 12/19/2017 by Minister Rhue Rosa for "Sister SOULdier"

Have you ever seen a wall
Not made by human hands?
It keeps all hurt and pain away
And lets in no man

My wall was carefully constructed
Designed to withstand force
I felt the need for this structure
As my life took its course

I was vulnerable and open
Too trusting and naïve
Too willing to give the benefit of the doubt
Too eager to believe

Each day I inspected it
Repaired each crack and crevice
I never ventured beyond the wall
And I allowed no one to visit

'Til one day I heard a sound
A whisper, nothing loud
It beckoned me to overcome-
It was the voice of God!

I mounted up with eagles' wings
Above my towering wall
The bricks disintegrated
As I responded to the call

Beyond the wall I saw young people
Bound by hand and foot
I spread my wings and sheltered them
As I did so the earth shook

Their shackles clattered to the ground
As each child was set free
And I realized that once I crushed my wall
A SOULdier was born in me!!!

N.U.M.B. Never Underestimate My Brilliance

Numb...the adjective that tells how I felt after years and
years of losing my loved ones
Numbed is the verb that tells what pain did to me
Sucked all my emotions...I have to tell someone!

I can't count the number of candles I've lit
The balloons I've released to a place I can't see
The t-shirts with names and faces and dates
If only memories could become living bodies

I had to make a choice about how to proceed
I have gifts, I have talents in spite of my wounds
I'll reflect on the greatness of each one I lost
And let that motivate me to rise from my tomb

I evict myself from the coffin of despair
Grateful for the times that I had with them all
Never underestimate my brilliance!!!
When winners are announced my name will be called!!

My brilliance is complex, it's multifaceted
It can't be measured, depleted nor drained
While I reminisce about great times we had
Depression evaporates and hope remains!

In their memory I'll press, persevere and succeed
I'll create, overflow, overcome and break free
I'll radiate in dark places, shine in obscurity
I can't be terminated. There's greatness in me!

By Minister Rosa, dedicated to those who lost loved ones
to gun violence, written 5/22/20

Oh, My Father!

I miss you more than words can express
Your wisdom, your knowledge, love and advice
You led by example, I learned so much
You gave me a foundation on which to build my life
Oh, my Father!
I am a physician and my job is to heal
But I have an ache that I could not cure
When I sit in my office and remember your voice
Sometimes the pain is more than I can endure
Oh, my Father!
My work is difficult, so many challenges
But I am YOUR daughter, I have your DNA
This means that GREATNESS flows through my veins
And because of YOU I am who I am today.

Written on 10/10/18 by
Rhue Rosa, LMSW for Dr. B.

Poem for Love Family by Minister Rhue Rosa

in silence you speak louder than thunder
in chaos your whisper is heard above all
in trials your power sustains and uplifts
in sorrow your love won't permit me to fall

like lightning you rip my doubts into shreds
assuring me that the devil can't harm me
you surround me with shields and hedges to guard me
angels though unseen wage war around me

time races on and cannot be grasped
seconds tic by until days have elapsed
watching and waiting for change and breakthrough
expectantly hoping and looking toward you

I stand at a crossroad, my paradigm shifting
the cares of this life have me slipping and drifting
your Word is the anchor that wont let me go
your blood is the substance that keeps me afloat

I declare and decree I'll come forth as pure gold
when I finish this race your glory I'll behold
so when it seems like I'm on the brink of despair,
I can rest assured knowing your presence is here

Poem for Mother Rosa

Whose hugs can melt a heart of ice and make a thug start crying?
Who can brighten up a room just by talking and smiling?
Whose cooking makes you feel as if you died and went to heaven?
Who always looks past our flaws and is always forgiving?
Mother Rosa is a special jewel...a diamond...a rare pearl
She brings her unique flavor to our corner of the world
What would our lives have been like without this Dominican Queen?
Mother Rosa you are the most precious woman our eyes have ever seen!

By Minister Rhue Rosa
8/16/2018

Vision, Voice and VICTORY!

A womb is a wonder
A hidden place
That shelters a life in darkness and warmth
BUT...the MOUTH is mysterious
Fixed on a face...
YET, out of it proceeds HOPE during storms
An anointed voice is a vehicle
That transports the hearer
From the depths of despair to the peak of peace
A praise can surmount obstacles
And overturn obstructions
Demons tremble when a melody of worship is released
May your Vision be supported
May your Voice flow unhindered
May your Victory be certain with no defeat in sight
As you exalt Him with harmony
Grace, gentleness and humility
May your birthday be a blessed one, continue the fight!

Birthday poem for co-worker
from Rhue Rosa, LMSW
written on 8/31/19

Dead to Sin

Christ cremated the OLD me!
I had trauma triggered by tragedy
It had warped, wounded and withered me
Till I was light years away from my destiny

I am born again because the birth route
Led from a heavenly matrix to divine truth
Dead to sin, dead to death...new worldview
In Christ I wreak havoc on demon crews

When prayer is fervent and power-packed
Evil spirits can't advance... they turn back!
No retreat, no surrender! Initiate attack!
I give NO PLACE to the enemy, not a crack!

I close the door to his schemes and devices
I don't bow down to him during crises
I lay aside doubt, depression and biases
DOOM is dead to me because Christ LIVES!

Written by Minister Rhue Rosa 6/11/2020

Pastor "Fire" Cole

I remember jerk chicken breasts and child care
Warnings and counsel to make me aware
Advice about life, satan's lies and God's blessings
You covering me with prayer- preventing me from
stressing

I remember the car lot on Eastern Parkway and Bushwick
Where you warned me about wolves in sheep's clothing
playing tricks
I remember you speaking to me here on Belmont
Tears flowed 'cause the Godly wisdom pricked my heart

I remember the talks after all-night prayer on Monroe
The therapy and psychiatry... who knew how much you
know???
You hold your tongue for no one
"Heartical Don" of all "dons"
Some THINK and claim they are "dons"
But they are DANDELIONS!

Compared to the ruffneck dignitary
Who doesn't run from adversity
You "pity party" with nobody
'Cuz you're charged to lead an army

Not an army of wimpy losers
Who retreat and surrender to challenge
This Black History Month I honor you
Pastor "Fire" Cole... you're a LIVING LEGEND!

By Minister Rhue Rosa 2/20/2020

I Nominate HOPE

I am trying to find a unique kind
Someone who'll embrace a renewed mind
End the epidemic of doubt in our brains
Get hooked on hope...bellow new refrains!
Receptive to life like a healthy womb
Resist defeat, denounce doom
We can't let our dreams die so soon!
There are always breakthroughs in the breaking news!
Shut down the oppressive mindsets
Let's embrace some hope and excitement
because we are ENDING the epidemic
Looking forward to building one another again
Just like "hope deferred makes the heart sick"
Good news of breakthroughs makes the heart tick
I'm campaigning for change in the district
Repair the glitch that was caused by doubt in our circuits
Darkness can't block the shine
Supernatural sight...
Eyes of faith see past time!
Belief builds courage and extinguishes fear
Hope distances defeat
and causes strength to draw near

I'm trying to find a format, a platform, an outlet
Which would arrest your attention
And ensure that you're aware that
Someone cares about you...
As a person, as an individual
And speaking of individuality
I hope you know your identity
Isn't only what your blood says about you
You have unique purpose
There's greatness in you...
I even see it on the surface!
So as you resume and return
To whatever you were doing
Before I caught your ear
Just remember...
That living with HIV/AIDS
Is no longer a death sentence
Our votes have been cast...they've been sent
Now we can declare with confidence
We're ending the epidemic!
I nominate HOPE for president!

By Rhue Rosa, LMSW
dedicated to HIV+ people

Heroes in the Home

Not ALL soldiers go away to war
And leave their loved ones behind..
Some spend each day on a battlefield...
Disarming bombs in a child's mind
A child who is in foster care
Confused, afraid, perplexed
Unsure of what is going on,
uncertain of what comes next...
As foster parents, you're a bridge
Though the future is unknown
children cross over and find themselves
In your stable, welcoming home
Foster parents are irreplaceable
You're heroes in disguise
You're healing, helping and tirelessly

Wiping tears from weeping eyes
As foster parents you play a role
That can't be truly measured
The work is hard but you don't quit
Because you're guarding treasure.
You're on the frontlines, often exhausted,
but fighting on nevertheless
No one can imagine how much you endure–
The challenges, trials, and the stress
So we honor you today and assure you
That in this walk you're never alone
We'll support you and ever appreciate you,
You are HEROES IN THE HOME!

By Rhue Rosa, LMSW

Tragedy is the Trigger

Tragedy... is the trigger that leads to the Hennessey
It's calling your name like a melody
'Cause you need an escape from the misery
What you don't realize... it's a fallacy!

You could drink the whole bottle, don't leave a drop
Your speech starts to slur and your head will bop
And if you do something violent here come the cops
So you're drowning in liquor...you need to stop!

I've been down that road, it's a dead end
I advise you to try what I recommend
I can't sit back and watch all the dough you spend
On something you'll just have to buy again

I can't see Hennessey being the remedy
Try The Rock, not Ciroc, you CAN break free!
Keep your dead loved ones in your memories
They would want you to live life abundantly

Not Ciroc, get The Rock, and that's JESUS
We won't run, never will, 'cause He frees us
No hangovers, just overflow, that's because
With Christ in our hearts we're victorious!!!

By Minister Rhue Rosa 5/31/2020

CPSIA information can be obtained
at www.ICGtesting.com
Printed in the USA
BVHW081924211121
622174BV00004B/85